NINJUTSU

AND

THE ARTICLES OF SUN TZU

孫 子 の 兵 法

LOST ARTS
PUBLICATIONS

NINJUTSU

AND

THE ARTICLES OF SUN TZU

A Re-Presentation of
Sun Tzu's Writings
as they appear in
The Book of War,

first translated from the Chinese in 1908 by
Captain E. F. Calthrop, R.F.A.

With a new Preface and
Commentary on Ninjutsu by
James Loriega
New York Ninpokai

LOST ARTS
PUBLICATIONS

First Printing: April 2018

ISBN: 978-1-387-74298-1

Lost Arts Publications
Brooklyn, NY 11235

LOST ARTS
PUBLICATIONS

Dedication

To those few who walk
the silent, secret path—*Shinobi-no Michi*—
guided by the *Sonshi-no-Heiho*

Taijutsu is great,
… but *Ninjutsu* will beat it—every time

Introduction to the Heihojin Collection

There is Wisdom in the Old Ways of the Shinobi ...

... and when the old ways are unknown—or worse, ignored—the wisdom they contain is lost. Among the many repositories where the old ways can be found are the seven classic military treatises of China, the *shinobi* writings of Iga and Koga, and the legacy strategies from master swordsmen of the Sengoku and Tokugawa eras.

Speaking very generally, the Chinese military treatises—diverse as they are—present insights into the adversary's motivations, concerns, and thinking. They provide, in essence, an understanding of the enemy's mind. Similarly, the shinobi writings of the 17th century provide a process for solving conventional situations through the use of unconventional tactics. And finally, the writings of Japanese swordsmen offer lucid insights into the development of a proper mindset, not merely for surviving life-and-death engagements involving razor-sharp steel, but more significantly for living life to the fullest in an environment where death might wait around the next bend in the road.

The latter sources are often disregarded because, in the thinking of many ninjutsu practitioners, there still exists a *false dichotomy* between what they discretely categorize as either "samurai" or "ninja" writings. Such practitioners overlook the fact that valuable philosophical strategies and tactical methods abound in the writings of samurai authors who, beyond simply being swordsmen, were in fact *master strategists—or heihojin!*

It matters not whether one practices kenjutsu, or even even includes sword work in one's training. What matters is the strategic thinking that these treatises and manuals contain for contending against an adversary. Such thinking remains timeless and relevant regardless of whether an encounter takes place on a battlefield, in a personal duel, or during a personal interaction. So learn, practice, and embrace the old ways—

The true *shinobi* never forfeits an advantage.

About the Publisher

Lost Arts Publications was established in 2015 to satisfy the growing interest in unique, rare, and almost-lost martial disciplines, arts, and systems. Niche-focused on lesser-known and rarely-seen methods, from both Eastern and Western perspectives, Lost Arts Publications produces original works in both hardcover and paperback formats.

Two imprints also publish under the Lost Arts Publications banner. The *Pay-Per-Cut Press* imprint specializes in edged weapons and systems of European origin. The *Raven Tradecraft* imprint focuses on modern spycraft and civilian tradecraft.

NINJUTSU

AND

THE ARTICLES OF SUN TZU

Contents

PREFACE

The beginnings of ninjutsu are not clear, but there can be no doubt that it is of Japanese origin, though it was greatly influenced by Chinese military spying techniques.

—Donn F. Draeger
Asian Fighting Arts

Like most readers, I became aware of Sun Tzu's classic teachings very early in life, but it was not until the mid-80s—well after I first opened my first dojo—that I began to fully understand the treatise's great influence on the *art of ninjutsu*. At the time I also served as Technical Editor for **Ninja** magazine and one of its owners, David Weiss, asked me about the relevance of Sun Tzu's book to the art I was teaching. My boilerplate answer, quoted from one of Donn Draeger's books, led to David proposing an article to me on the subject. It was then I began reading the heretofore unopened copy of **The Art of War** that sat on my shelf, and noting the correlations between the dicta of Sun Tzu and the tenets of ninjutsu.

It is necessary to clarify here that the Chinese title of Sun Tzu's treatise is **Sunzi Bingfa** (孫子兵法). *Sunzi* refers to the author, Master Sun, which is written as "Sun Tzu" in English and other Western languages. The term *Bingfa*, however, can have multiple meanings and has been more arbitrarily translated, depending on the particular translator's perspective.

Thus, it turns out that the two men who first translated the *Sunzi Bingfa* into English approached the process differently. Captain E. F.

11

Calthrop—who produced the present translation—was a British officer stationed in Tokyo when he published his work, calling it **The Book of War**. Dr. Lionel Giles, the translator of the more widely-available interpretation that most readers are familiar with, was a highly accomplished linguist and scholar in Chinese culture. He called his work, **The Art of War**. Since becoming familiar with those two works, I continued to collect, read, and dissect subsequent editions and translations of Sun Tzu's classic writings and came to realize just how much a translator's *perspective* influences his work.

My purpose in assembling this edition of Captain E. F. Calthrop's **Book of War** is threefold: first, to underscore the fact that rarely is one perspective the *only* way to interpret a thing (especially the art of ninjutsu, which we all claim to "understand"); second, to present a view of Sun Tzu's work that is different—neither better nor worse—from the one we may already have read, especially with respect to strategy, ninjutsu, and its philosophical evolution; and third, to provide those not familiar with any translation with an expanded understanding of the roots of the ninja's art.

—James Loriega
New York City 2018

Introductory Comments

Ninjutsu is supposed to have originated more than 2,000 years ago as a treatise on the art of spying in the ancient Chinese book on military science...

—Andrew Adams
Ninja, The Invisible Assassins

The military treatise we today call *The Art of War* was introduced to Japan around 735 AD by *Kibi-no-Makibi,* a Japanese scholar and noble who resided in China for almost twenty years. The most literal rendering of the title **Sunzi Bingfa (孫子兵法)** in English is actually "Master Sun's Way of Warfare." *Sun,* of course, was the author's given name, and *Tzu,* an honorific for a learned individual, similar to *Master,* or *Doctor* in the academic sense. *Fa,* sometimes written *fah,* means "way of" or "method of." The familiar Japanese equivalent of *fa* is *po,* as in *Kenpo* or *Ninpo. Bing,* sometimes written *ping,* refers to the *weapons used in war* and, by extension, its use implies *warfare.*

Sun Tzu, Sunzi, Sonbu, and Sonshi

The treatise quickly became popular among Japanese generals and military clan leaders who began to plumb the depths of the military strategies it contained. However, while the Japanese could read the Chinese characters, their pronunciation of the terms in the treatise was "accented" in their own native language.

Inevitably, the names of the author and of the treatise became transliterated: Sun Tzu's name, which sometimes appeared as **Sun Wu** (meaning *Sun* from *Wu,* his home province), was read as **Sonbu** in

13

Japan. Similarly his treatise, the *Sunzi Bingfa*, became known simply as the **Sonshi**, the Japanese pronunciation of *Sunzi*. The Japanese word *heiho*, or "strategy," was later added to the title for specificity, and the work was henceforth known as the **Sonshi-no-Heiho**, or the "Strategies of Sunzi."

The Book of War or The Art of War

All of the above *shades of meaning* were deemed to be too nuanced for two unrelated British translators—Captain E. F. Calthrop and Dr. Lional Giles—who, understandably, required a simpler title for their English-speaking readers. Thus it was that **The Book of War** and **The Art of War** became the treatise's initial titles, with the latter sounding slightly more lofty to the sophisticated ear.

Crouching Tiger, Hidden Dragon, and Limiting Views

On December 8, 2000, I was invited to attend the premiere screening of *Crouching Tiger, Hidden Dragon* at New York City's Lincoln Center. Director Ang Lee, along with Chow Yun-Fat, Michelle Yeoh, Zhang Ziyi, and other stars from the film were also present. Following the film's viewing, the director and cast were bought back on-stage to engage in a question-and-answer session with members of the entertainment media. The very first question, posed specifically to Ang Lee, was, "What was your main challenge in producing this film?" Without pausing to think, Ang Lee replied, "The most difficult challenge I faced came from the fact that *talented actors don't know how to fight, and talented fighters don't know how to act.*"

Mr. Lee's observation is analogous to what occurred with the early English translations of the *Sunzi Bingfa*: Captain Calthrop, a professional militarist, lacked the exacting linguistic ability possessed by Dr. Lionel Giles; Giles, in turn, lacked Calthrop's—or any—military experience and perspective. And while some may say that Giles' lack of a military background is of no consequence, it must be borne in mind that the *Sunzi Bingfa* is, after all, a text on *military* strategy, and that Giles was, by his own words, translating the work for members of the academic community. His translation, though commonly accepted as the definitive one, has also been deemed flawed, predictably, by later translators and linguistic scholars within the military.

Untangling Mysterious Theads and The Divine Skeins

Having said that, it would also be a mistake to assume that the more contemporary translators are without their own shortcomings. To demonstrate this point I'll use Sun Tzu's last chapter, (from which the Japanese abtracted the concept of ninjutsu), as an example. This chapter's title has alternately been translated as the "Using Spies," "The Employment of Secret Agents," "The Divine Manipulation of the Threads," "The Mysterious Thread," and "The Divine Skein."

The word *skein*—meaning *a loosely bundled length of thread or yarn*--was deliberately utilized by Sun Tzu in the 7th and 8th lines of the chapter. He picked the word to connote a variety of spies who, while deceptively appearing to be random or unrelated, are in fact connected to the same general or ruler in a manner not easily discernible to the unsuspecting enemy.

Calthrop translates the lines in question as:

> 7. *Now the five kinds of spies are these: village spies, inner spies, converted spies, death spies, living spies.*
> 8. *If these five means be employed simultaneously, none can discover their working. This is called The Mysterious Thread.*

Giles translates them as:

> 7. *Hence the use of spies, of whom there are five classes: local spies; internal spies; turned spies; expendable spies; surviving spies.*
> 8. *When these five kinds of spy are all at work, none can discover the secret system. This is called the divine manipulation of the threads.*

Yet General Samuel B. Griffith, whose translation of *The Art of War* I otherwise regard to be the most accurate, interprets the significance of *the Divine Skein* quite differently from what Sun Tzu probably meant. In a footnote within his translation, Griffith opines:

> *The idea is that information may be gathered in as fish are by pulling on a single cord and so drawing in together the various threads of a net.*

This is poetic, but unlikely; and that footnote repesents one section of the treatise where General Griffith was not translating but rather speculating—and his interpretation is, in my view, a *misinterpretation*.

But interestingly, the much-maligned Calthrop clearly understood the implicit meaning of the "threads" or "skein" when, with regard to spies, he notes,

> *The spy was treated with great honor by his country-men, and the fact that many of the national heroes of China were spies shows that the part they played was not forgotten. They frequently toiled for years, and rose to high rank in the enemy's service; and thus, by wrong*

counsel and by spreading mistrust in his ranks, they became a two-edged sword in the hands of the general.

As I read it, the *toiling spy* that Calthrop describes is comparable to a "thread" in the fabric of *the enemy's service*; woven in, I would venture, to "unravel" the enemy's defenses. Griffith, to be certain, was a highly experienced officer with an unrivaled command of Chinese in its literal and figurative forms, but it is doubtful that his extensive military expertise extended to the realm of ninjutsu, which is at the heart of the Thirteenth Chapter.

Hard Facts and Subtle Meanings

There are, of course, many other hard facts and subtle meanings that surround Master Sun's treatise, its adoption by Japan's *bushi* and *shinobi* cultures, and its translation into Western languages. Those topics, however, are covered in exhaustive detail in **Ninjutsu and the Art of War**, a companion volume to this, and are not replicated here, where the focus is specifically on Calthrop's translation, exclusive of Giles'.

—JL

Notes Regarding This Edition:

The original publication of **The Book of War** consists of two translations by Capt. E. F. Calthrop: the first is of *The Articles of Sun Tzu*; the second is of *The Sayings of Wu Tzu*. The *Sayings* are not included in this edition because, though they also address military strategy, they do not relate directly to Sun Tzu or his writings.

The text of Capt. Calthrop's translation appears in this edition exactly as it was published in 1908. No words or text have been added or deleted, revised, or edited.

I have also resisted the impulse to footnote or annotate within the Calthrop's text. All footnotes are his own.

Misspellings have not been corrected.

THE FOLLOWING PAGES, (17-88), CONTAIN CAPT. CALTHROP'S FULL
AND ORIGINAL TRANSLATION OF *THE ARTICLES OF SUN TZU*
AS THEY APPEAR IN **THE BOOK OF WAR**

THE
BOOK OF WAR

The Military Classic
Of The Far East

Translated From The Chinese By
Captain E. F. Calthrop, R.F.A.

London
JOHN MURRAY, ALBEMARLE ST., W.
1908

The Book of War

Introduction

I

WRITTEN in the fifth century B.C., Suntzu and Wutzu still remain the most celebrated works on war in the literature of China. While the chariot has gone, and weapons have changed, these ancient masters have held their own, since they deal chiefly with the fundamental principles of war, with the influence of politics and human nature on military operations; and they show in a most striking way how unchanging these principles are.

When these books were written, China was a conglomerate of principalities in continual ferment. Personal ambition and intrigue, and not the wishes of the people, were the main factors in these wars. Patriotism, or a popular cause, could not, therefore, be relied on to maintain the moral of the levies. Instead of these, what may be called the force of despair is pointed out as the most powerful agent in giving cohesion and energy to an army. The general is urged to take a vigorous offensive; and to act at a distance from his base, where defeat means disaster, and where desertion is minimised owing to the distance from home. He should, in fact, burn his boats before an action, or, in Chinese phrase, act as one who removes the ladder from under those mounted upon the roof.

On the other hand, every care must be taken not to render the enemy desperate; and, as an instance of this, Sun observes that an opponent should on no account be completely surrounded. A loop-hole of escape weakens the resolution of the general and the energy of his troops.

It is interesting to notice that moral, or the spirit of the troops, is thus considered a determining factor in war. The Chinese are perhaps unusually affected by climatic conditions. As is well known, the umbrella was part of a soldier's equipment; and for the same reasons, the sunny side of high ground is recommended as most suitable for defence, tactical considerations permitting.

The large number of bannermen in the Chinese army was out of all proportion to the service of standards in providing rallying points. The chief use of banners was to maintain the spirit of the troops. A forest of banners, held erect, gave a feeling of liveliness and security to the ranks, in the same way as a military band, and when Sun remarks that the march of an army should be calm like the forest, he is using a simile that is not inappropriate.

Probably owing to the fact that the profession of arms has never been highly regarded in China, we find that the ruler of the state did not usually take the field, but employed a professional to command the army—one of the masters of war who wandered from state to state at that time with the secrets of victory to impart to the highest bidder. The question of political interference with the general in the field naturally arises under these conditions. The two sages point out, that to unite the nation under firm and just government is the business of the ruler and necessary to victory; but that the general is the best judge of the questions that arise on a distant field, and that all interference with him causes delay and disaster.

War meaning ravage, it was essential that the operations should be conducted in the enemy's territory. Once there, however, a vigorous offensive is no longer advised. "At first behave with the discretion of a maiden" is the counsel of Sun. The enemy must be induced to take the initiative, and when he is worn out by marching, or makes a false move, "then," says the master, "dart in like a rabbit."

Unlike the tactics of the Japanese, in whom the spirit of attack burns so strongly, those of Suntzu and Wutzu are essentially of the offensive-defensive order—manœuvre before fighting, and non-committal until the enemy has shown his hand. The business of the general is to avoid encounter in battle until the enemy is no longer capable of offering a successful resistance.

The masters do not make, however, the mistake of advocating a passive defensive. Suntzu lays down that the division of the forces which this strategy involves, is to be everywhere weak, rendering the army liable to be taken in detail by the concentrated forces of the

23

enemy. It is rather the defence which avoids battle by mobility and manœuvre, induces the enemy by stratagem to divide his forces, or act in conformity with our wishes, and then falls upon him.

With regard to the tactics of the battlefield, the pitched battle, or, in other words, the frontal attack, is considered unworthy of the skilful general. The plan of attack should consist, broadly speaking, in the division of the army into two forces. The enemy is "attracted and engaged by one force, and defeated with the other;" and here we have the containing or secondary attack, and the main or reserve force which decides the battle of to-day—a most striking instance of the continuity of military principles.

Considerable space is devoted to the influence of ground on war. The passage of defiles and rivers is still conducted in the same way. The many large rivers of China naturally affected military operations; and, among other axioms, it is laid down that the passage of a river should not be disputed, as the enemy will probably give up the attempt, and make the passage untouched at some other point, but that he should be attacked when half his force is across the stream. Again, an army should not encamp on a river below the enemy, as it is thereby liable to be inundated, or to have its water poisoned; or the enemy may come down stream and make a sudden attack.

While both writers were professional soldiers, they show a fine disinterestedness by repeatedly pointing out that even successful war brings evil in its train. Wu remarks that "few are those who have gained power on earth by many victories," and he is insistent that war should not be undertaken until a careful comparison of the two sides shows that victory is certain; and he adds, "The army which conquers makes certain of victory and then attacks, while the army that is defeated fights in the hope of success."

Hence the importance they assign to intelligence of the enemy, and to the spy; and as the sages dealt with war between members of the same race, the work of spies was greatly facilitated. The spy was treated with great honour by his countrymen, and the fact that many of the national heroes of China were spies, shows that the part that they played was not forgotten. They frequently toiled for years, and rose to high rank in the enemy's service; and thus, by wrong counsel and by spreading mistrust in his ranks, they became a two-edged sword in the hands of the general. "Wonderful, indeed, is their power," exclaims Sun; but he also reminds us that their management is the most difficult and delicate duty of the general.

II

Sun and Wu are perhaps held in even greater reverence in Japan than in China, where war is looked upon as a troublesome phase in national life, and victory in battle is not considered the greatest achievement of a state. Far otherwise is it in Japan; and successive generations of her soldiers have been brought up on Sun and Wu. Like other arts, mystery was formerly supposed to surround the art of war, a belief that was encouraged by the strategist; and for a considerable time, the few copies of this book, that were brought over from China to Japan, were jealously guarded by their possessors. Later, as they became known, an army of Japanese commentators arose—for Chinese literature is thought compressed, to be unfolded in the mind of the reader.

To-day Sun and Wu have given way to the scientific works of European writers, but their sayings have become proverbs, and their influence undoubtedly helped the Japanese to victory in the late war. Belief in the importance of a knowledge of the enemy and his resources, of preparation and training, had grown out of a long study of these ancient masters; and since it was the vital importance of a successful issue to the Japanese which, after all, fired their resolution and carried them through, they proved the sage's words that it is the energy, born of despair, that wins the victory.

III

Little is known of the life of either master. They were in no sense patriots but professional strategists, continually changing their employer. Chinese history tells a famous story about Sun. A certain ruler asked Sun to give a practical demonstration of his principles in the neighbourhood of the palace, and entrusted him with the women of the court for this purpose. During the operations, the leader of one of the sides did not obey the master's instructions, and her execution was ordered. She happened to be the king's favourite wife, but Sun pointed out that the king's wish that her life should be spared was a case of political interference with the general in the field; and the sentence was carried out.

Wu is represented as a person of low moral character. On two separate occasions, for fear of giving rise to suspicion, he killed one of his wives who belonged to a state with which his employer at the time was at war; and, graver still in the eyes of the Chinese historian, he was not present at the death-bed of his mother.

E. F. C.

NOTE.

The translator is indebted to Major J. C. Somerville
for his kind help and criticism.

I

PRELIMINARY RECKONING

The words of Sun the Master:—

To all nations War is a great matter. Upon the army death or life depend: it is the means of the existence or destruction *of the State*. Therefore it must be diligently studied.

Now, in war, besides stratagem and the situation, there are five indispensable matters. The first is called The Way[1]; the second, Heaven; the third, Earth; the fourth, the Leader; the fifth, Law.

The Way or the proper conduct of man. If the ruling authority be upright, the people are united: fearless of danger, their lives are at the service of their Lord.

Heaven. Yin and Yang[2]; heat and cold; time and season.

Earth. Distance; nature; extent; strategic position.

The Leader. Intelligence; truth; benevolence; courage and strictness.

Law. Partition and ordering of troops.

These things must be known by the leader: to know them is to conquer; to know them not is to be defeated.

---

1 The five virtues of humanity, righteousness, propriety, wisdom, and faith are known as The Way.

2 The Yin and Yang are the two principles into which natural phenomena are divided in Chinese philosophy. Yin is the masculine, active, or light principle, and Yang is the feminine, passive, or dark principle. In this connection, day and night, rain, mist and wind are designated.

Further, with regard to these and the following seven matters, the condition of the enemy must be compared with our own.

The seven matters are:—

> The virtue of the prince;
>
> the ability of the general;
>
> natural advantages;
>
> the discipline of the armies;
>
> the strength of the soldiers;
>
> training of the soldiers;
>
> justice both in reward and punishment.

Knowing these things, I can foretell the victor.

If a general under me fight according to my plans, he always conquers, and I continue to employ him; if he differ from my plans, he will be defeated and dismissed from my service.

Wherefore, with regard to the foregoing, considering that with us lies the advantage, and the generals agreeing, we create a situation which promises victory; but as the moment and method cannot be fixed beforehand, the plan must be modified according to circumstances.

War is a thing of pretence: therefore, when capable of action, we pretend disability; when near to the enemy, we pretend to be far; when far away, we pretend to be near.

Allure the enemy by giving him a small advantage. Confuse and capture him. If there be defects, give an appearance of perfection, and awe the enemy. Pretend to be strong, and so cause the enemy to avoid you. Make him angry, and confuse his plans. Pretend to be inferior, and cause him to despise you. If he have superabundance of strength, tire him out; if united, make divisions in his camp. Attack weak points, and appear in unexpected places.

These are the secrets of the successful strategist, therefore they must not be made known beforehand.

At the reckoning in the Sanctuary before fighting, victory is to the side that excels in the foregoing matters. They that have many of these will conquer; they that have few will not conquer; hopeless, indeed, are they that have none.

If the condition of both sides with regard to these matters be known, I can foretell the victor.

II

OPERATIONS OF WAR

Sun the Master said:—

Now the requirements of war are such that we need a thousand light chariots with four horses each; a thousand leather-covered chariots, and one hundred thousand armoured men; and we must send supplies to distant fields. Wherefore the cost at home and in the field, the entertainment of guests, glue and lacquer for repairs, and necessities for the upkeep of wagons and armour are such that in one day a thousand pieces of gold are spent. With that amount a force of one hundred thousand men can be raised:—you have the instruments of victory.

But, even if victorious, let the operations long continue, and the soldiers' ardour decreases, the weapons become worn, and, if a siege be undertaken, strength disappears.

Again, if the war last long, the country's means do not suffice. Then, when the soldiers are worn out, weapons blunted, strength gone and funds spent, neighbouring princes arise and attack that weakened country. At such a time the wisest man cannot mend the matter.

For, while quick accomplishment has been known to give the victory to the unskilful, the skilful general has never gained advantage from lengthy operations.

In fact, there never has been a country which has benefited from a prolonged war.

He who does not know the evils of war will not reap advantage thereby. He who is skilful in war does not make a second levy, does not load his supply wagons thrice.

War material and arms we obtain from home, but food sufficient for the army's needs can be taken from the enemy.

The cost of supplying the army in distant fields is the chief drain on the resources of a state: if the war be distant, the citizens are impoverished.

In the neighbourhood of an army prices are high, and so the money of the soldiers and followers is used up. Likewise the state funds are exhausted, and frequent levies must be made; the strength of the army is dissipated, money is spent, the citizen's home swept bare: in all, seven-tenths of his income is forfeited. Again, as regards State property, chariots are broken, horses worn out, armour and helmet, arrow and bow, spear, shield, pike and fighting tower, wagon and oxen used and gone, so that six-tenths of the Government's income is spent.

Therefore the intelligent general strives to feed on the enemy; one bale of the enemy's rice counts as twenty from our own wagons; one bundle of the enemy's forage is better than twenty of our own.

Incitement must be given to vanquish the enemy.

They who take advantage of the enemy should be rewarded.

They who are the first to lay their hands on more than ten of the enemy's chariots should be rewarded; the enemy's standard on the chariots exchanged for our own; the captured chariots mixed with our own chariots and taken into use.

The accompanying warriors must be treated well, so that, while the enemy is beaten, our side increases in strength.

Now the object of war is victory; not lengthy operations, even skilfully conducted.

The good general is the lord of the people's lives, the guardian of the country's welfare.

III

THE ATTACK BY STRATAGEM

Sun the Master said:—

Now by the laws of war,

Better than defeating a country by fire and the sword, is to take it without strife.

Better to capture the enemy's army intact than to overcome it after fierce resistance.

Better to capture the "Lu[3]," the "Tsu" or the "Wu" whole, than to destroy them in battle.

To fight and conquer one hundred times is not the perfection of attainment, for the supreme art is to subdue the enemy without fighting.

Wherefore the most skillful warrior outwits the enemy by superior stratagem; the next in merit prevents the enemy from uniting his forces; next to him is he who engages the enemy's army; while to besiege his citadel is the worst expedient.

A siege should not be undertaken if it can possibly be avoided. For, before a siege can be commenced, three months are required for the construction of stages, battering-rams and siege engines; then a

---

3 The Chinese army consisted of 12,500, the " lu" of 500," tsu" of 50, and the "wu " of 5 men.

further three months are required in front of the citadel, in order to make the "Chuyin[4]." Wherefore the general is angered, his patience exhausted, his men surge like ants against the ramparts before the time is ripe, and one-third of them are killed to no purpose. Such are the misfortunes that sieges entail.

Therefore the master of war causes the enemy's forces to yield, but without fighting; he captures his fortress, but without besieging it; and without lengthy fighting takes the enemy's kingdom. Without tarnishing his weapons he gains the complete advantage.
This is the assault by stratagem.

By the rules of war, if ten times as strong as the enemy, surround him; with five times his strength, attack; with double his numbers, divide. If equal in strength, exert to the utmost, and fight; if inferior in numbers, manœuvre and await the opportunity; if altogether inferior, offer no chance of battle. A determined stand by inferior numbers does but lead to their capture.

The warrior is the country's support. If his aid be entire, the country is of necessity strong; if it be at all deficient, then is the country weak.

---

4 The "Chuyin" was a large tower or work constructed to give command over the interior of the enemy's fortress. High poles were also erected, from the top of which archers, each encased in an arrow-proof box and raised by a rope and pulley, shot at the besieged.

Now a prince may embarrass his army in three ways, namely:—

Ignorant that the army in the field should not advance, to order it to go forward; or, ignorant that the army should not retreat, order it to retire. This is to tie the army as with a string.

Ignorant of military affairs, to rule the armies in the same way as the state. This is to perplex the soldiers.

Ignorant of the situation of the army, to settle its dispositions.

This is to fill the soldiers with distrust.

If the army be perplexed and distrustful, then dangers from neighbouring princes arise. The army is confounded, and offered up to the enemy.

There are five occasions when victory can be foretold:—

when the general knows the time to fight and when not to fight;
or understands when to employ large or small numbers;
when government and people are of one mind;
when the state is prepared, and chooses the enemy's unguarded moment for attack;
when the general possesses ability, and is not interfered with by his prince.

These five things are the heralds of victory.

It has been said aforetime that he who knows both sides has nothing to fear in a hundred fights; he who is ignorant of the enemy, and fixes his eyes only on his own side, conquers, and the next time is defeated; he who not only is ignorant of the enemy, but also of his own resources, is invariably defeated.

IV

THE ORDER OF BATTLE

Sun the Master said:—

The ancient masters of war first made their armies invincible, then waited until the adversary could with certainty be defeated.

The causes of defeat come from within; victory is born in the enemy's camp.

Skilful soldiers make defeat impossible, and further render the enemy incapable of victory.

But, as it is written, the conditions necessary for victory may be present, but they cannot always be obtained.

If victory be unattainable, we stand on the defensive; if victory be sure, we attack.

Deficiency compels defence; super-abundance permits attack.

The skilful in defence crouch, hidden in the deepest shades; the skilful in attack push to the topmost heaven[5].

---

5 Literally 9th heaven, and 9th earth. The Chinese divided the earth and sky each into 9 strata

If these precepts be observed, victory is certain.

A victory, even if popularly proclaimed as such by the common folk, may not be a true success. To win in fight, and for the kingdom to say, "Well done," does not mark the summit of attainment. To lift an autumn fleece[6] is no proof of strength; the eyes that only see the sun and moon are not the eagle's; to hear the thunder is no great thing.

As has been said aforetime, the able warrior gains the victory without desperate and bloody engagements, and wins thereby no reputation for wisdom or brave deeds. To fight is to win, for he attacks only when the enemy has sown the seeds of defeat.

Moreover, the skilful soldier in a secure position does not let pass the moment when the enemy should be attacked.

The army that conquers makes certain of victory, and then seeks battle.

The army destined to defeat, fights, trusting that chance may bring success to its arms.

The skilful leader is steadfast in the "Way"; upholds the Law, and thereby controls the issue.

---

6 An animal's coat is thinnest in autumn.

Touching the laws of war, it is said: first, the rule; second, the measure; third, the tables; fourth, the scales; fifth, the foretelling of victory.

For the rule is the survey of land; the measure tells the amount of that land's produce; the tables its population; from the scales their weight or quality is made known; and then can we calculate victory or defeat. The army that conquers as against the army destined to defeat, is as a beam against a feather in the scales. The attack of conquering forces is as the outburst of long-pent-up waters into sunken valleys.

Such are the orders of battle.

V

THE SPIRIT OF THE TROOPS

Sun the Master said:—

The control of large numbers is possible, and like unto that of small numbers, if we subdivide them.

By means of drum, bell and flag[7], the direction of large forces in battle is possible, and like unto the direction of small forces.

By the skilful interchange of normal and abnormal manœuvres are the armies certainly preserved from defeat.

The enemy is crushed, like the fall of a grindstone upon an egg, by knowledge of his strength and weakness, and by the employment of truth and artifice.

Moreover, in battle the enemy is engaged with the normal and defeated by the abnormal force[8].

---

7 The drum was used to beat the assembly and in the advance, the bell as a signal to halt. Flags were of two kinds, signaling flags and distinguishing banners.

8 The normal and the abnormal refer to what in modern phrase are termed the frontal or holding force and the flanking or surprise force.

The abnormal force, skilfully handled, is like the heaven and earth, eternal; as the tides and the flow of rivers, unceasing; like the sun and moon, for ever interchanging; coming and passing, as the seasons.

There are five notes; but by combinations, innumerable harmonies are produced. There are but five colours; but if we mix them, the shades are infinite. There are five tastes, but if we mix them there are more flavours than the palate can distinguish[9].

In war there are but two forces, the normal and the abnormal; but they are capable of infinite variation. Their mutual interchange is like a wheel, having neither beginning or end. They are a mystery that none can penetrate.

As the rush of rock-shouldering torrents, so is the spirit of the troops.

Like the well-judged flight of the falcon, in a flash crushing its quarry, so should the stroke be timed.

Wherefore the spirit of the good fighter is terrifying, his occasions sudden; like the stretched cross-bow, whose string is released at the touch of the trigger.

In the maze and tumult of the battle, there is no confusion; in the thick of action the battle array is impenetrable.

---

9 The five cardinal tastes are, acridity, bitterness, sourness, sweetness and saline taste.

If discipline be perfect, disorder can be simulated; if truly bold, we can feign fear; if really strong, we can feign weakness.

We simulate disorder by subdivision; fear, by spirit; weakness, by battle formation.

We set the enemy in motion by adopting different formations to which he must conform.

If we offer the enemy a point of advantage, he will certainly take it: we give him an advantage, set him in motion and then fall upon him.

Wherefore the good fighter seeks victory from spirit, and does not depend entirely upon the skill of his men. He is careful in his choice, and leaves the rest to battle force; yet, when an opening or advantage shows, he pushes it to its limits.

As a log or rock which, motionless on flat ground, yet moves with ever-increasing force when set on an incline, so await the opportunity, and so act when the opportunity arrives.

If the general be skillful, the spirit of his troops is as the impetus of a round stone rolled from the top of a high mountain.

VI

EMPTINESS AND STRENGTH

Sun the Master said:—

To be the first in the field, and there to await the enemy, is to husband strength.

To be late, and hurrying to advance to meet the foe, is exhausting.

The good fighter contrives to make the enemy approach; he does not allow himself to be beguiled by the enemy.

By offering an apparent advantage, he induces the enemy to take up a position that will cause his defeat; he plants obstructions to dissuade him from acting in such a way as to threaten his own dispositions.

If the enemy be at rest in comfortable quarters, harass him; if he be living in plenty, cut off his supplies; if sitting composedly awaiting attack, cause him to move.

This may be done by appearing where the enemy is not, and assaulting unexpected points.

If we go where the enemy is not, we may go a thousand leagues without exhaustion.

If we attack those positions which the enemy has not defended, we invariably take them: but on the defence we must be strong, even where we are not likely to be attacked.

Against those skillful in attack, the enemy does not know where to defend: against those skillful in defence, the enemy does not know where to attack.

Now the secrets of the art of offence are not to be easily apprehended, as a certain shape or noise can be understood, of the senses; but when these secrets are once learnt, the enemy is mastered.

We attack, and the enemy cannot resist, because we attack his insufficiency; we retire, and the enemy cannot pursue, because we retire too quickly.

Again, when we are anxious to fight, but the enemy is serenely secure behind high walls and deep moats; we attack some such other place that he must certainly come out to relieve.

When we do not want to fight, we occupy an unfortified line; and prevent the enemy from attacking by keeping him in suspense.

By making feints, and causing the enemy to be uncertain as to our movements, we unite, whilst he must divide.

We become one body; the enemy being separated into ten parts. We attack the divided ten with the united one. We are many, the enemy is few, and in superiority of numbers there is economy of strength.

The place selected for attack must be kept secret. If the enemy know not where he will be attacked, he must prepare in every quarter, and so be everywhere weak.

If the enemy strengthen his front, he must weaken his rear; if he strengthen his right, his left is weakened; and if he strengthen his left, his right is weakened.

Everywhere to make preparations, is to be everywhere weak. The enemy is weakened by his extended preparations, and we gain in strength.

Having decided on the place and day of attack, though the enemy be a hundred leagues away, we can defeat him.

If the ground and occasion be not known, the front cannot help the rear; the left cannot support the right, nor the right the left, nor the rear the front. For on occasion, the parts of the army are two score leagues apart, while a distance of four or five leagues is comparatively close.

The soldiers of Wu[10] are less than the soldiers of Yueh; but as superiority in numbers does not of necessity bring victory, I say, then, that we may obtain the victory.

If the enemy be many in number, prevent him from taking advantage of his superiority, and ascertain his plan of operations. Provoke the enemy and discover the state of his troops; feint and discover the strength of his position. Flap the wings, and unmask his sufficiency or insufficiency. By constant feints and excursions, we may produce on the enemy an impression of intangibility, which neither spies nor art can dispel.

The general makes his plans in accordance with the dispositions of the enemy, and puts his hosts in motion; but the multitude cannot appreciate the general's intention; they see the signs of victory, but they cannot discover the means.

If a victory be gained by a certain stratagem, do not repeat it. Vary the stratagem according to circumstances.

An army may be likened to water.
Water leaves dry the high places, and seeks the hollows. An army turns from strength and attacks emptiness.

The flow of water is regulated by the shape of the ground; victory is gained by acting in accordance with the state of the enemy.

10 Sun, as has been said, was a man of Wu. Wu and Yueh were continually at war.

The shape of water is indeterminate; likewise the spirit of war is not fixed.

The leader who changes his tactics in accordance with his adversary, and thereby controls the issue, may be called the God of war.

Among the five elements[11] there is no settled precedence; the four seasons come and go; the days are long and short; and the moon waxes and wanes. So in war there is no fixity.

---

11 Wood, fire, earth, metal and water

VII

BATTLE TACTICS

Sun the Master said:—

For the most part, military procedure is as follows:—
The general receives orders from his lord; assembles and settles harmony among the forces, and takes the field.

There is nothing more difficult than Battle Tactics. Their difficulty lies in the calculation of time and distance, and the reversal of misfortune.

To make the enemy take a circuitous route by a show of gain, and then, whilst starting after him, to arrive before him, is to be a master of the art of manœuvre.

The operations of an army may reap advantage; the wrangles of a multitude are fraught with peril.

Employing our whole force at one time in order to gain advantage over the enemy, we may not have time enough to gain our object. If we push on with a portion of the force only, the transport is lost. Discarding helmet and armour; stopping neither day nor night; marching double distance; doing double work; and finally contending with the enemy at a distance of a hundred leagues: results in the loss of the general. Since the strong men arrive first, and the tired drop in rear, only one-tenth of the forces is available.

A forced march of fifty leagues to secure an advantage may result in failure to the leader of the vanguard, for only half his men will arrive.

After a forced march of thirty leagues to secure an advantage, only two-thirds of the army will be available.

Further, a lack of ammunition, of supplies, or of stores, may lead to disaster.

The ruler who is ignorant of the designs of neighbouring princes, cannot treat with them.

He who is ignorant of mountain and forest, defile and marsh, cannot lead an army.

He who does not employ a guide, cannot gain advantage from the ground.

Disguise your movements; await a favourable opportunity; divide or unite according to circumstance.

Let your attack be swift as the wind; your march calm like the forest[12]; your occupation devastating as fire. In defence, as a mountain rest

---

12 This passage was written on the standard of Takeda Shingen, one of Japan's most famous generals

firm; like darkness impenetrable to the enemy. Let your movements be swift as the lightning.

Let as many as possible take part in the plunder: distribute the profit from the captured territory.

So he who understands the crooked and the straight way conquers.

These are the methods of Battle Tactics.

According to the ancient books on war, the drum and bell are used, because the voice does not carry; the flag is used to assist the sight. The use of bell, drum, banner and flag is to attract the united attention of eye and ear.

When all are united, the strong are not left to go forward alone, the cowardly are not free to retreat unrestricted. In this way can a multitude be used.

Therefore in night fighting, beacons and drums are largely used; in day fighting, a great number of banners and flags and the enemy's eyes and ears are confounded.

We thus awe his army, and defeat his general's ambition.

In the morning the spirits are keen; at midday there is a laziness; in the evening a desire to return. Wherefore, he who uses his soldiers well, avoids the time when the spirits are keen; but attacks the enemy when he is languid or seeking his camp.

Thus should the nature of energy be turned to account.

To oppose confusion with order, clamour with quiet, is to have the heart under control.

To await an enemy from a distance, to oppose hunger with satiety, rest with fatigue, is the way to husband strength.

Do not attack where lines of banners wave, nor the serried ranks of battle spread, but patiently await your time.

Do not attack an enemy on high ground, nor one who has high ground at his back. Do not pursue an enemy who is imitating flight; do not attack a spirited enemy.

If the enemy offer an allurement, do not take it.

Do not interfere with an enemy who has struck camp, and is about to retire. When surrounding an enemy, allow him an outlet. Do not press a desperate enemy.

These are the methods of employing troops.

VIII

THE NINE CHANGES

Sun the Master said:—

In general, the procedure of war is:—the Leader, having received orders from his lord, assembles the armies.

Do not camp on marshy or low-lying ground; enter into friendly relations with neighbouring states; do not linger in a far country; use stratagem in mountainous and wooded country; on death ground, fight.

There are always roads that must be avoided; forces that must not be attacked; castles that must not be besieged; ground that must not be chosen for encounter; orders from the lord that must not be obeyed.

The general who knows the Nine Changes understands the use of troops; on the contrary, he who does not understand them, can make no use of his topographical knowledge.

In the management of armies, if the art of the Nine Changes be understood, a knowledge of the Five Advantages is of no avail.

The wise man considers well both advantage and disadvantage. He sees a way out of adversity, and on the day of victory to danger is not blind.

In reducing an enemy to submission, inflict all possible damage upon him; make him undertake useless adventures; also make neighbouring rulers move as you would desire them by tempting them with gain.

Wherefore in the conduct of war do not depend on the enemy's not coming, but rely on your own preparations; do not count on the enemy not attacking your fortress, but leave nothing undefended.

Generals must be on their guard against these five dangerous faults:—
    Blind impetuosity, which leads to death.
    Over-cautiousness, which leads to capture.
    Quick temper, which brings insult.
    A too rigid propriety, which invites disgrace.
    Over-regard for the troops, which causes inconvenience.

These five faults in the leader are disastrous in war. The overthrow of the army and the slaughter of the general arise from them. Therefore they must be carefully considered.

IX

Movement of Troops

Sun the Master said:—

Touching the disposal of troops and observation of the enemy in relation to mountain warfare:—

Cross mountains and camp in valleys, selecting positions of safety.

Place the army on high ground, and avoid an enemy in high places.

In relation to water:—

After crossing waters, pass on immediately to a distance. When the enemy is crossing a stream, do not meet and engage him in the waters, but strike when half his force has passed over. Do not advance on an enemy near water, but place the army on high ground, and in safety.

Do not fight when the enemy is between the army and the source of the river.

With regard to marshes:—

Cross salty marshes quickly; do not linger near them.

If by chance compelled to fight in the neighbourhood of a marsh, seek a place where there is water and grass, and trees in plenty in the rear.

In open country place the army in a convenient place with rising ground in the right rear; so that while in front lies death, behind there is safety.

Such is war in flat country.

Huangti, by observing these things, gained the victory over four Princes.

As a rule, the soldiers prefer high ground to low. They prefer sunny places to those the sun does not reach.

If the health of the troops be considered, and they are encamped on high and sunny ground, diseases will be avoided, and victory made certain.

If there be rising ground, encamp on its sunny side and in front of it; for thereby the soldiers are benefited, and the ground used to our advantage.

If, owing to rains in the upper reaches, the river become turbulent, do not cross until the waters have quieted.

Steep and impassable valleys; well-like places; confined places; tangled impenetrable ground; swamps and bogs; narrow passages with pitfalls: —quickly pass from these, and approach them not. Cause the enemy to approach near to them, but keep yourself from these places; face them, so that the enemy has them in his rear.

If there be near to the army, precipices, ponds, meres, reeds and rushes, or thick forests and trees, search them thoroughly. These are places where the enemy is likely to be in ambush.

When the enemy is close, but quiet, he is strong in reliance on natural defences.

If the enemy challenge to fight from afar, he wishes you to advance.

If the enemy be encamped in open country, it is with some special object in view.

Movement among the trees shows that the enemy is advancing. Broken branches and trodden grass, as of the passing of a large host, must be regarded with suspicion.

The rising of birds shows an ambush.

Startled beasts show that the enemy is stealthily approaching from several sides.

High, straight spurts of dust betoken that chariots are coming.

Long, low masses of dust show the coming of infantry.

Here and there, thin and high columns of dust are signs that firewood and fodder are being collected.

Small clouds of dust moving to and fro are signs that the enemy is preparing to encamp for a short time.

Busy preparations and smooth words show that the enemy is about to advance to attack.

Big words, and the spurring forward of horsemen, are signs that the enemy is about to retire.

An advance of the light chariots to the flanks of the camp is a sign that the enemy is coming forth to fight.

Without consultation, suddenly to desire an armistice, is a mark of ulterior design.

The passing to and fro of messengers, and the forming up of troops, show that the enemy has some movement on foot.

An advance, followed by sudden retirement, is a lure to attack.

When the enemy use their weapons to rest upon, they are hungry.

If the drawers of water drink at the river, the enemy is suffering from thirst.

Disregard of booty that lies ready at hand is a sign of exhaustion.

The clustering of birds round a position shows that it is unoccupied.

Voices calling in the night betoken alarm.

Disorder in the army is a sign that the general is disregarded.

A changing about of flags and banners is a sign that the army is unsettled.

If the officers be angry, it is because the soldiers are tired, and slow to obey.

The killing of horses for food shows that the enemy is short of provisions.

When the cooking-pots are hung up on the wall and the soldiers turn not in again, the enemy is at an end of his resources.

Exceeding graciousness and familiarity on the part of the general show that he has lost the confidence of the soldiers.

Frequent rewards show that discipline is at an end.

Frequent punishments are a sign that the general is in difficulties.

The general who first blusters, and then is obsequious, is without perception.

He who offers apologies and hostages is anxious for a truce.

When both sides, eager for a fight, face each other for a considerable time, neither advancing nor retiring, the occasion requires the utmost vigilance and circumspection.

Numbers are no certain mark of strength.

Even if incapable of a headlong assault, if the forces be united, and the enemy's condition ascertained, victory is possible.

He who without taking thought makes light of the enemy is certain to be captured.

If a general who is strange to the troops punish them, they cease to obey him. If they are not obedient, they cannot be usefully employed.

If the troops know the general, but are not affected by his punishments, they are useless.

By humane treatment we obtain obedience; authority brings uniformity. Thus we obtain victory.

If the people have been trained in obedience from the beginning, they respect their leader's commands.

If the people be not early trained to obedience, they do not respect their leader's commands.

Orders are always obeyed, if general and soldiers are in sympathy.

X

GROUND

Sun the Master said:—

With regard to the different natures of ground there are:—

Open ground; broken ground; suspended ground; defiles; precipices; far countries.

Open ground is that where either side has liberty of movement: be quick to occupy any high ground in the neighbourhood and consider well the line of supplies.

Broken ground. Advance is easy, but retreat from it is difficult. Here, if the enemy be not prepared, we may win: but should he be prepared, and defeat us, and retreat be impossible, then there is disaster.

Suspended ground. The side that takes the initiative is under a disadvantage. Here, if the enemy offer some allurement, we should not advance: but rather, by feigning retreat, wait until he has put forth half his force. Then we may attack him with advantage.

Defiles, make haste to occupy; garrison strongly and await the enemy. Should the enemy be before you, and in strength, do not engage him; but if there be unoccupied points, attack him.

In precipitous ground quickly occupy a position on a sunny height, and await the enemy. If the enemy be before you, withdraw and do not attack him.

If distant from the enemy, and the forces be equal, to take the initiative is disadvantageous.

Now, these are the six kinds of ground. It is the duty of generals to study them.

Again, there are six calamities among the troops, arising, not from defect of ground, or lack of opportunity, but from the general's incapacity. These are:

> repulse,
> relaxation,
> distress,
> disorganisation,
> confusion and
> rout.

If troops be sent to attack an enemy of equal quality, but ten times their number, they retire discomfited.

Strong soldiers with weak officers cause relaxation.

Able officers with feeble soldiers cause distress.

Enraged senior officers, who fall upon the enemy without orders, and obey not the general because he does not recognise their abilities, produce disorganisation.

Weak and amiable generals, whose directions and leadership are vague, whose officers' and men's duties are not fixed, and whose dispositions are contradictory, produce confusion.

Generals, who are unable to estimate the enemy, who oppose small numbers to large, weakness to strength, and who do not put picked men in the van of the army, cause it to be routed.

These six things lead to defeat. It is the duty of the general to study them carefully.

Ground is the handmaid of victory.

Ability to estimate the enemy, and plan the victory; an eye for steepness, command and distances: these are the qualities of the good general.

Whosoever knows these things, conquers; he who understands them not, is defeated.

If victory be certain from the military standpoint, fight, even if the lord forbid.

If defeat be certain from the military standpoint, do not fight, even though the lord commands it.

The general who advances, from no thought of his own glory, or retires, regardless of punishment; but only strives for the people's welfare, and his lord's advantage, is a treasure to the state.

The good general cares for his soldiers, and lovingly treats them as his children; as a consequence they follow him through deep valleys, and are beside him in death.

Nevertheless, over-care for the soldiers may cause disobedience; over-attention may make them unserviceable; over-indulgence may produce disorder: they become like spoilt children, and cannot be used.

He who is confident of his own men, but is ignorant that the enemy should not be attacked, has no certainty of victory.

He who knows that the enemy may be attacked with advantage, but knows not his own men, has no certainty of victory.

Confidence in the troops, right judgment when to attack the enemy, but ignorance of the ground, bring uncertain victory.

The wise soldier, once in motion, does not waver, and is never at a loss.

As has been said: *"Know thyself; know the enemy; fear not for victory."*

Also, if the season and the opportunity be realised, and the ground known, complete victory is certain.

XI

THE NINE GROUNDS

Sun the Master said:—

In respect to the conduct of war there are:—
Distracting ground; disturbing ground; ground of contention; intersecting ground; path-ridden ground; deeply-involved ground; difficult ground; enclosed ground; death ground.

At all times, when the prince fights in his own territory, it is called distracting[13] ground.

That ground a short way inside the enemy's border is called disturbing ground.

Ground giving advantage to whichever side is in possession, is called ground of contention.

Ground to which either side has access, is called intersecting ground.

Ground between three provinces first possession of which enables the peoples of the earth to be controlled, is called path-ridden ground.

---

13 This and the following are so called because the men are continually thinking of, and slipping back to their homes.

The interior of the enemy's country with many of his fortified towns in rear, is called deeply-involved ground.

Mountain and forest, precipices, ravines, marsh and swamp, all places where passage is hard, are called difficult ground.

A narrow entrance and winding outlet, where a small number can oppose a large force, is called enclosed ground.

That ground where delay means disaster, is called death ground.

Wherefore, do not fight on distracting ground; do not linger on disturbing ground.

If the enemy be in possession of disputed ground, do not attack.

In intersecting ground, do not interrupt the highways.

At the crossing of highways, cultivate intercourse.

When deeply involved, levy and store up the enemy's property.

Quickly depart from difficult ground.

On enclosed ground, use stratagem.

On death ground, fight.

The skillful fighters of old were at pains to disconnect the enemy's front and rear; they cut asunder small and large forces of the enemy; prevented mutual help between his officers and men; spread mistrust between high and low. They scattered the enemy, and prevented him from concentrating; if his soldiers were assembled, they were without unity.

If there be a chance of victory, move; if there be no chance of success, stand fast.

If I were asked how a powerful and united force of the enemy should be met, I would say: lay hands on what the enemy cherishes and he will conform to our desires.

In war, above all, speed sustains the spirit of the troops. Strike before the enemy is ready; and attack his unpreparedness from an unexpected quarter.

With regard to war in foreign lands. When strangers in a far country the soldiers are united and are proof against defeat. Plunder fertile plains so that the army is fed; be careful of the health of the soldiers; do not tire them uselessly; unite their minds; store up strength; plan well and secretly. If there be no refuge the soldiers will not fly from death.

If there be no alternative but death, the soldiers exert themselves to the utmost.

In desperate places, soldiers lose the sense of fear.

If there be no place of refuge, there will be no wavering.

If deeply involved in the enemy's country, there is unity.

If it be unavoidable, the soldiers will fight their hardest. Even without warnings they are vigilant; they comply without insistence; without stipulations they are tractable; without explicit instructions they will trust the general and obey him.

Prohibit the discussion of signs and omens, and remove the soldiers' doubts; then to the moment of death they will be undistracted.

Riches are denied the soldiers, not because money is a bad thing; old age is forbidden them, but not because long life is evil. Hardships and danger are the proper lot of the soldier.

When the order for attack is given, the collars of those who are sitting may be wet with tears; tears may roll down the cheeks of those reclining; yet these men, in a desperate place, will fight with the courage of Chu and Kuei.

Soldiers should be used like the snakes on Mt. Chang; which, if you hit on the head, the tail will strike you; if you hit the tail, the head will strike you; if you strike its middle, head and tail will strike you together.

Should any one ask me whether men can be made to move like these snakes, I say, yes. The men of Wu and Yueh hate each other; yet, if they cross a river in the same boat and a storm overtake them, they help each other like the two hands.

The horses may be tied, and the chariot wheels sunk in the mud; but that does not prevent flight.

Universal courage and unity depend on good management.

The best results from both the weak and strong are obtained by a proper use of the ground.

The skillful warrior can lead his army, as a man leads another by the hand, because he places it in a desperate position.

The general should be calm, inscrutable, just and prudent. He should keep his officers and men in ignorance of his plans, and inform no one of any changes or fresh departures. By changing his camps, and taking devious and unexpected routes, his plans cannot be guessed.

As one taking away the ladder from under those mounted upon the roof, so acts the general when his men are assembled to fight. He penetrates into the heart of the enemy's country and then divulges his plans. He drives the army hither and thither like a flock of sheep, knowing not whither they go.

Therefore the general should assemble the armies, and place them in a desperate position.

The different natures of the Nine Grounds; the suiting of the means to the occasion; the hearts of men: these are things that must be studied.

When deep in the interior of a hostile country, there is cohesion; if only on the borders, there is distraction. To leave home and cross the borders is to be free from interference.

> On distracting ground, unite the soldiers' minds.
> On disturbing ground, keep together.
> On disputed ground, try to take the enemy in rear.
> On intersecting ground, look well to the defences.
> On path-ridden ground, cultivate intercourse.
> On deeply-involved ground be careful of supplies.
> On difficult ground, do not linger.
> On enclosed ground, close the path of escape.
> On death ground, show the soldiers that there is no chance of survival.

It is the nature of soldiers to defend when surrounded, to fight with energy when compelled thereto, to pursue the enemy if he retreat.

He cannot treat with other rulers who knows not their ambitions.

He who knows not mountain and forest; cliffs; ravines; lakes and marshes; cannot conduct an army.

He who does not use guides, cannot take advantage of the ground.

He who has not a complete knowledge of the Nine Grounds, cannot gain military dominion.

The great general, when attacking a powerful nation, prevents the enemy from concentrating his hosts.

He overawes the enemy so that other states cannot join against him.

He does not struggle for the favour of other states; nor is he careful of their rights. He has confidence in himself, and awes the enemy.

Therefore he easily takes the fortress, or reduces the country to subjection.

In the bestowal of rewards, or in his orders, he is not bound by ancient rule.

He manages his forces as though they were one man.

Orders should direct the soldiers; but while what is advantageous should be made known, what is disadvantageous should be concealed.

If the forces be plunged into danger, there is survival; from death ground there is retrieval; for the force in danger gains the victory.

Discover the enemy's intentions by conforming to his movements. When these are discovered, then, with one stroke, the general may be killed, even though he be one hundred leagues distant.

When war is declared, close the barriers; destroy passports; prevent the passage of the enemy's spies; conduct the business of the government with vigilance.

Take immediate advantage of the enemy's weakness; discover what he most values, and plan to seize it.

Shape your plans according to rule, and the circumstances of the enemy.

At first behave with the discretion of a maiden; then, when the enemy gives an opening, dart in like a rabbit.

The enemy cannot defend himself.

XII

ASSAULT BY FIRE

Sun the Master said:—

There are five ways of attack by fire:

> The first is called barrack burning;
>
> the second, commissariat burning;
>
> the third, equipment burning;
>
> the fourth, store burning;
>
> the fifth, the company burning.

The moment for the fire assault must be suitable. Further, appliances must always be kept at hand.

There is a time and day proper for the setting and carrying out of the fire assault; namely: such time as the weather is dry; and a day when the moon is in the quarters of the stars Chi, Pi, I, Chen: for these are days of wind.

Regard well the developments that will certainly arise from the fire, and act upon them. When fire breaks out inside the enemy's camp, thrust upon him with all speed from without; but if his soldiers be quiet, wait, and do not attack.

When the fire is at its height, attack or not, as opportunity may arise.

If the opportunity be favourable, set fire to the enemy's camp, and do not wait for it to break out from within.

When fire breaks out on the windward side, do not attack from the leeward.

Wind that rises in the day lasts long. Wind that rises in the night time quickly passes away.

The peculiarities of the five burnings must be known, and the calendar studied, and, if the attack is to be assisted, the fire must be unquenchable.

If water is to assist the attack, the flood must be overwhelming.

Water may isolate or divide the enemy; fire may consume his camp; but unless victory or possession be obtained, the enemy quickly recovers, and misfortunes arise. The war drags on, and money is spent.

Let the enlightened lord consider well; and the good general keep the main object in view. If no advantage is to be gained thereby, do not move; without prospect of victory, do not use the soldiers; do not fight unless the state be in danger.

War should not be undertaken because the lord is in a moment of passion. The general must not fight because there is anger in his heart.

Do not make war unless victory may be gained thereby; if there be prospect of victory, move; if there be no prospect, do not move.

For passion may change to gladness, anger passes away; but a country, once overturned, cannot be restored; the dead cannot be brought to life.

Wherefore it is written, the enlightened lord is circumspect, and the good general takes heed; then is the state secure, and the army victorious in battle.

XIII

THE EMPLOYMENT OF SPIES

Sun the Master said:—

Calling 100,000 men to arms, and transporting them a hundred leagues, is such an undertaking that in one day 1,000 taels of the citizens' and nobles' money are spent; commotions arise within and without the state; carriers fall down exhausted on the line of march of the army; and the occupations of 700,000[14] homes are upset.

Again, for years the armies may face each other; yet the issue may depend on a single day's victory.

Wherefore, by grudging slight expense in titles and salaries to spies, to remain in ignorance of the enemy's circumstances, is to be without humanity. Such a person is no general; he is no assistance to his lord; he is no master of victory.

The enlightened ruler and the wise general who act, win, and are distinguished beyond the common, are informed beforehand.

---

14 The population was divided, for military purposes, into groups of eight families. In time of war, each group sent one man into the field, furnished his wants, and provided for his family. Therefore if 100,000 men are taken, 700,000 homes are affected.

This knowledge is not to be got by calling on gods and demons; nor does it come of past experience nor calculation. It is through men that knowledge of the enemy is gained.

Now the five kinds of spies are these:

    village spies,

    inner spies,

    converted spies,

    death spies,

    living spies.

If these five means be employed simultaneously, none can discover their working. This is called the *Mysterious Thread*: it is the Lord's Treasure.

    Village spies are such people of the country as give information.

    Inner spies are those of the enemy's officials employed by us.

    Converted spies are those of the enemy's spies in our pay.

    Death[15] spies are sent to misinform the enemy, and to spread false reports through our spies already in the enemy's lines.

    Living spies[16] return to report.

---

15 So called because they are put to death when the enemy finds out that he has been tricked.

16 Messengers and others, who do not disguise their identity, are included under this heading.

In connection with the armies, spies should be treated with the greatest kindness; and in dealing out reward, they should receive the most generous treatment. All matters relating to spies are secret.

Without infinite capacity in the general, the employment of spies is impossible. Their treatment requires benevolence and uprightness. Except they be observed with the closest attention, the truth will not be obtained from them.

Wonderful indeed is the power of spies.
There is no occasion when they cannot be used.

If a secret matter be spoken of before the time is ripe, the spy who told the matter, and the man who repeated the same, should be put to death.

If desirous of attacking an army; of besieging a fortress; or of killing a certain person; first of all, learn the names of the general in charge; of his right-hand[17] men; of those who introduce visitors to the Presence; of the gate keeper and the sentries. Then set the spies to watch them.

Seek out the enemy's spies who come to spy on us; give them money; cause them to be lodged and cared for; and convert them to the service. Through them we are enabled to obtain spies among the enemy's villagers and officials.

---

17 Literally, right and left men, i.e., *they who sat on either side.*

By means of the converted spy, we can construct a false story for the death spy to carry to the enemy.

It is through the converted spy that we are able to use the five varieties, to their utmost advantage; therefore he must be liberally treated.

In ancient times the rise to power of the province of Yin was due to Ichih, who was sent to the country of Hsia. Likewise during the foundation of the state of Chu, Luya lived among the people of Shang. Wherefore, intelligent rulers and wise generals use the cleverest men as spies, and invariably acquire great merit. The spy is a necessity to the army. Upon him the movement of the army depends.

THIS MARKS THE END OF
CAPT. CALTHROP'S TRANSLATION OF
THE ARTICLES OF SUN TZU

THE THIRTEENTH CHAPTER

The ninja have a very long history indeed, with their origins to be found in Ancient China ... Sun Tzu's account of the use of spies, in which he sketches out much of what has become recognised as ninja-lore, forms the thirteenth chapter of his work.

—Stephen Turnbull
Ninja, The True Story of
Japan's Secret Warrior Cult

Although it falls outside the scope of this book to provide a comprehensive, side-by-side comparison of the E.F. Calthrop (1908) and Lionel Giles (1910) translations, I have opted to include, below, Dr. Giles' rendering of the Thirteenth Chapter. That final chapter of the treatise is of major significance to many because—

- it formally validates the importance of espionage for the survival of the State;

- it elevates the role of the espionage agent to a level above the rest of the State's military forces; and

- it codifies the requisite qualities and responsibilities of each type of spy.

A careful reading of the Thirteenth Chapter's subtext also provides direction to the spymaster—whether he be the commander of the military or the ruler of the State—for the efficient management of the spies serving under him.

Japanizing the Treatise

For ninjutsu practitioners, the Thirteenth Chapter represents the first milestone in the documented timeline of the art; if not in specific techniques, then certainly in timeless principles. As Draeger writes in one of his books, most foreign concepts that reach Japan become improved and, as he puts it, ultimately "Japanized." In this instance, the Japanese began as avid students of Sun Tzu's various theories and quickly rose to become masters in their application.

THE USE OF SPIES
from Lionel Giles' *The Art of War*

Sun Tzu said:

Raising a host of a hundred thousand men and marching them great distances entails heavy loss on the people and a drain on the resources of the State. The daily expenditure will amount to a thousand ounces of silver. There will be commotion at home and abroad, and men will drop down exhausted on the highways. As many as seven hundred thousand families will be impeded in their labor.

Hostile armies may face each other for years, striving for the victory which is decided in a single day. This being so, to remain in ignorance of the enemy's condition simply because one grudges the outlay of a hundred ounces of silver in honors and emoluments, is the height of inhumanity.

One who acts thus is no leader of men, no present help to his sovereign, no master of victory.

Thus, what enables the wise sovereign and the good general to strike and conquer, and achieve things beyond the reach of ordinary men, is foreknowledge.

Now this foreknowledge cannot be elicited from spirits; it cannot be obtained inductively from experience, nor by any deductive calculation.

Knowledge of the enemy's dispositions can only be obtained from other men.

Hence the use of spies, of whom there are five classes.

Local spies

Internal spies

Turned spies

Expendable spies

Surviving spies

When these five kinds of spy are all at work, none can discover the secret system. This is called The Divine Manipulation of the Threads. It is the sovereign's most precious faculty.

Having local spies means employing the services of the inhabitants of a district.

Having internal spies, making use of officials of the enemy.

Having turned spies, getting hold of the enemy's spies and using them for our own purposes.

Having expendable spies, doing certain things openly for purposes of deception, and allowing our spies to know of them and report them to the enemy.

Surviving spies, finally, are those who bring back news from the enemy's camp.

Hence it is that which none in the whole army are more intimate relations to be maintained than with spies. None should be more liberally rewarded. In no other business should greater secrecy be preserved.

Spies cannot be usefully employed without a certain intuitive sagacity.

They cannot be properly managed without benevolence and straight-forwardness.

Without subtle ingenuity of mind, one cannot make certain of the truth of their reports.

Be subtle! be subtle! and use your spies for every kind of business.

If a secret piece of news is divulged by a spy before the time is ripe, he must be put to death together with the man to whom the secret was told.

Whether the object be to crush an army, to storm a city, or to assassinate an individual, it is always necessary to begin by finding out the names of the attendants, the aides-de-camp, and door-keepers and sentries of the general in command. Our spies must be commissioned to ascertain these.

The enemy's spies who have come to spy on us must be sought out, tempted with bribes, led away and comfortably housed. Thus they will become turned spies and available for our service.

It is through the information brought by the turned spy that we are able to acquire and employ local and internal spies.

It is owing to his information, again, that we can cause the expendable spy to carry false tidings to the enemy.

Lastly, it is by his information that the surviving spy can be used on appointed occasions.

The end and aim of spying in all its five varieties is knowledge of the enemy; and this knowledge can only be derived, in the first instance, from the turned spy. Hence it is essential that the turned spy be treated with the utmost liberality.

Of old, the rise of the Yin dynasty was due to I Chih who had served under the Hsia. Likewise, the rise of the Chou dynasty was due to Lu Ya who had served under the Yin.

Hence it is only the enlightened ruler and the wise general who will use the highest intelligence of the army for purposes of spying and thereby they achieve great results. Spies are a most important element in water, because on them depends an army's ability to move.

AFTERWORD

It bears noting that those historical individuals who today are known to have been followers of the Sonshi-no-Heiho are the same ones whose decisions and actions were pivotal to the rise of Japan as a nation; among them, Minamoto Yoshitsune, Kusunoki Masahige, Yamamoto Kansuke, Takeda Shingen, Oda Nobunaga, and Tokugawa Ieyasu.

Yamamoto, Takeda, and the Sonshi

Yamamoto Kansuke, perhaps the greatest strategist of the *Sengoku* era, became Takeda's mentor in his study of the Sonshi, and also served as spymaster to Takeda's network of ninja. Yamamoto's own treatise on military strategy, the **Heiho Okugi-sho**, should rank just below the Sonshi as required reading for ninjutsu practitioners.

Subsequently, Yamamoto's apt pupil (and employer), Takeda Shingen, drew the inspiration for his famous battle cry—*Fuurin Kazan*—from the Seventh chapter of the Sonshi.

> *Let your attack be swift as the wind;*
> *your march calm like the forest:*
> *your occupation devastating as fire.*
> *In defence, as a mountain rests firm;*
> *like darkness impenetrable to the enemy.*
> *Let your movements be swift as the lightning.*

Takeda, a military genius by all accounts, is also reputed to have established two discrete systems of ninjutsu: one was focused on actual intelligence-gathering methods; the other, equally if not more significantly, was focused on the *transmission methods* of intelligence. Takeda realized that the information obtained by his spies was useless if it did not reach decision-makers in an expeditious or timely manner. To ensure this happened, he devised a series of transmission methods —also taken from the Seventh chapter of the Sonshi.

> *According to the ancient books on war,*
> *the drum and bell are used, because the voice does not carry;*
> *the flag is used to assist the sight.*
> *The use of bell, drum, banner and flag*
> *is to attract the united attention of eye and ear.*

Takeda simply took the methods prescribed for the battlefield and developed ways to utilize them in the less clamorous conditions of covert espionage.

Closing Thoughts

The fact that Giles' translation of Sun Tzu's writing is by far the better of the two in question is beyond dispute; but that fact alone should not in any way render Calthrop's translation as being without worth. Consider this—although many ninjutsu practitioners may speak and read Chinese[18] fluently, statistically most do not. If such is the case, and if you are within the majority that is not fluent, the question to ask yourself is:

Had Dr. Giles never produced his acclaimed translation of the Sonshi, would I find any benefit in Captain Calthrop's "flawed" translation?

What is important for us to understand is that while every translation has its inevitable deficits, there are great benefits to be derived by not obsessing on their perceived flaws and, instead, seeing—and learning from—the relative strengths of each.

It is my hope that ninjutsu practitioners unfamiliar with these works will see how Calthrop and Giles each approached the subject of utilizing spies, and get a sense of how the treatise's final, Thirteenth Chapter served as the framework for the codified espionage art that today some call *ninjutsu*.

---

18 By this I simply mean that those Chinese-fluent ninjutsu practitioners would be the only ones to potentially learn the strategies residing in the *Sunzi Bingfa*.

孫子の兵法

ADDENDA

The addenda which follow contain information relative the topics discussed in the preceding chapters. Their inclusion here is intended to assist ninjutsu practitioners in better understanding the thinking of the original author—and his early British translators—as it pertains to espionage, as well as to the art of ninjutsu.

SUN TZU
孙子
Author of The Art of War

Sun Tzu was a general and military strategist who is thought to have lived during China's *Spring and Autumn period* (776–471 BC). His birth name was **Sun Wu**, from which his Japanese name, *Sonbu*, is derived. The name *Sun Tzu*, by which he is most commonly known in the West, is an honorific meaning, "Master Sun." Other names used are *Sun-Zi* and *Sun Wu Tzu*.

Sonbu is traditionally credited as the author of the **Bingfa**, a widely influential work on military strategy that has impacted both Western and Eastern thinking. Also known as *The Thirteen Chapters*, the English-language name for this is **The Book of War** (Calthrop's translation) and **The Art of War** (all other translations.)

Little is certain regarding Sonbu, and the oldest available sources disagree as to where he was was born. The historian Szuma Chien, whose writings date back to the early 1st century B.C., describes Sonbu as a contemporary of Confucius. Some arguments against Sonbu's existence claim that, had such a great military mind existed, more would have been written of him than just passing references. Yet there are many entries in works from that time, accepted as historically accurate, which are given the same brief treatment.

Translator Samuel B. Griffith suggests that Sonbu probably lived during China's *Warring States period*[19], a time of constant war among seven Chinese nations[20] that fought to control the vast expanse of fertile territory in Eastern China. It was Sonbu's victories then that

---

19 453-221 B.C.
20 *Zhao, Qi, Qin, Chu, Han, Wei,* and *Yan.*

inspired him to write *The Art of War*. Translator Ralph Sawyer likewise believes it is very likely Sonbu did exist and also wrote the core of the book that bears his name.

We can be almost certain, therefore, that a man named Sun Tzu did exist and was the author of the book which bears his name. Until further evidence comes to light, the debate cannot be resolved; however, whether an individual called "Sun Tzu" existed in history is not as important as the work which has made that name famous— a work that in turn inspired the birth of the *art of ninjutsu*.

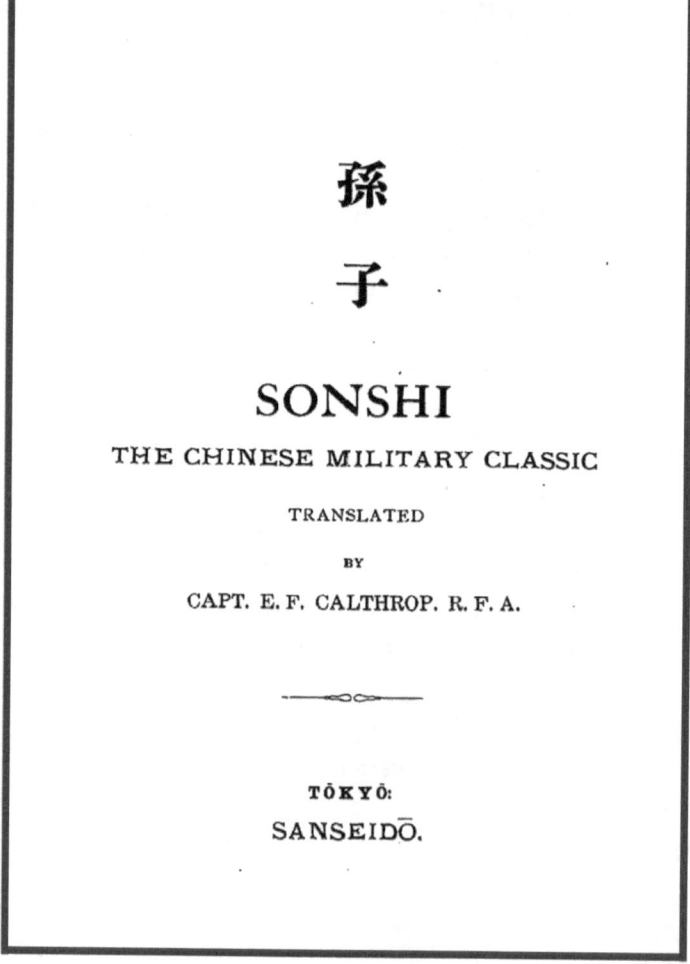

孫

子

SONSHI

THE CHINESE MILITARY CLASSIC

TRANSLATED

BY

CAPT. E. F. CALTHROP. R. F. A.

TÔKYÔ:

SANSEIDŌ.

Captain E. F. Calthrop, R.F.A.

Literary and academic circles have been harsh in their commentary of **The Book of War**, and more so of its translator, E. F. Calthrop. His successor, Dr. Lionel Giles, who titled his translation **The Art of War**, was particularly critical, writing of Calthrop in his Introduction,

> ... it was evident that the translator's knowledge of Chinese was far too scanty to fit him to grapple with the manifold difficulties of Sun Tzŭ. He himself plainly acknowledges that without the aid of two Japanese gentlemen "the accompanying translation would have been impossible." We can only wonder, then, that with their help it should have been so excessively bad.

In fact, one of Giles's own biographers, John Minford, has this to say:

> Giles' recurring and often ill-tempered broadsides against the unfortunate Captain Calthrop and his flawed 1908 translation (he almost seems to have been emulating his notoriously irascible and often petulant father) are the only feature that mars and dates an otherwise splendid book. This defect is not to be found in his other writings.

Rather than piece together a more objective and less scathing profile of Sun Tzu's first English-language translator, I have inserted instead below an obituary written by one of Calthrop's colleagues who, while probably not impartial, at least presents a more complete picture of the man.

The writing is unattributed and addressed to the Editor of THE SPECTATOR, dated 12 FEB 1916.

THE LATE MAJOR E. F. CALTHROP, R.F.A.

I venture to send you a short account of Major (temporary Lieutenant-Colonel) Everard Ferguson Calthrop, R.F.A., who fell in action in Flanders in December last, because your paper is one which reaches many distant parts of the world where his friends are to be found, and for whom, perhaps, it may be the only published record they will see, and also because a few years ago he contributed at least one remarkable article on Japan to your columns.

England has lost in Major Calthrop not only a keen and able soldier, but she has lost in him much more—namely, one of the most brilliant Oriental scholars of the younger generation, and the translator of the celebrated Chinese **Book of War,** that "Military Classic of the Far East" written in the Fifth century BC by the " Masters " *Sun* and *Wu*.

Major Calthrop entered the Army from Woolwich in 1895, and served through the Boer War with distinction, taking part in the relief of Ladysmith and receiving two medals and seven clasps. In January, 1904, he went to Japan as one of the first party of English officers sent to study the Japanese language and Army. He stayed four years, and was the only officer admitted to the Japanese Staff College. In 1908 he returned to England, and wars given a nomination to the Staff College, where he passed two years, after which he held an appointment in the Far Eastern Section of the War Office until 1914. In this year he was appointed Military Attache to Tokio, and he had started for Japan just before war broke out, arriving in time to be present at the siege of Tsing-tao. For some months he sought in vain for permission to return to Europe in order to go to the front. Finally this was given him, and he started in April, 1915, in a cargo-boat. He was kept in England until the end of September, when he left for Flanders, where he met his death on Sunday morning, December 19th.

Although, in the words of his mother, "he would not have wished a different end," one cannot but feel that it was questionable wisdom to send a man of his calibre to the trenches, thus risking the loss to the nation of a rare, and indeed in some ways unique, brain and personality. Of the sacred grief, borne with noble courage, of his mother and sister I cannot speak.

He was the only son of a widow, and the devotion of the little family of three to one another was a beautiful thing to witness. I can only speak of him as a friend who admired and loved him for his rare qualities of character and mind, and who counted it a great privilege to be admitted to his friendship. His was indeed a nature of wonderful sweetness, and his most striking characteristic was his peculiar gentle courtesy—a characteristic which has come to be called old-fashioned in a world where every one seems to be in a hurry. In him was found the strange and delightful combination of eager, youthful alertness, coupled with an almost diffident modesty and a complete absence of self-assertion. It was perhaps this combination which gave him, in full measure, that rare and most coveted gift of the gods—charm—and which won him hosts of friends without his ever consciously exerting himself to gain them. Even the Japanese, who are notoriously shy of according their confidence and friendship to a European, welcomed him, and admitted him into the intimacy of their home life in a way that they have done to very few of his countrymen.

The son of an accomplished artist, whose early death alone prevented him from achieving a wider reputation, Major Calthrop inherited great artistic gifts from his father, and there is little doubt that if his chosen profession had been that of art, he would have won distinction in any branch of it. As it was his strenuous soldier's life left him little time to cultivate his gifts to the full ; but in spite of this he was a line craftsman, and his delicate and refined taste was shown in many exquisitely artistic products of an unusual character, such as decorative bookbinding in the Japanese style. Among the numerous deplorable losses the nation has suffered in the premature extinction of so many of its finest specimens of chivalrous manhood, not the least deplorable is that of Major Calthrop. To his friends the sense of personal loss is deep and abiding, and they can but comfort themselves as best they may with the thought that as far as he is concerned— *"Nothing is here for tears . . . nothing but well and fair, And what may quiet us in a death so noble."*

DR. LIONEL GILES

Lionel Giles was a British sinologist, writer, and philosopher. He served as assistant curator at the British Museum and Keeper of the Department of Oriental Manuscripts and Printed Books. Giles is most notable for his 1910 translation of *The Art of War* by Sun Tzu and *The Analects of Confuciu*s.

Giles was born at Sutton, the fourth son of British diplomat and sinologis Herbert Giles and his first wife Catherine Fenn. Educated privately in Belgium (Liège), Austria (Feldkirch), and Scotland (Aberdeen), Giles studied Classics at Wadham College, Oxford, graduating BA in 1899.

The 1910 Giles translation of *The Art of War* succeeded British officer Everard Ferguson Calthrop's 1905 and 1908 translations, and refuted large portions of Calthrop's work. In his Introduction, Giles writes:

> It is not merely a question of downright blunders, from which none can hope to be wholly exempt. Omissions were frequent; hard passages were willfully distorted or slurred over. Such offenses are less pardonable. They would not be tolerated in any edition of a Latin or Greek classic, and a similar standard of honesty ought to be insisted upon in translations from Chinese.

Lionel Giles used the Wade-Giles romanization method of translation, pioneered by his father, Herbert Giles. Like many sinologists in the Victorian and Edwardian eras, he was primarily interested in Chinese literature, which was approached as a branch of classics. Victorian sinologists contributed greatly to problems of textual transmission of the classics.

Continuing to produce translations of Chinese classics well into the later part of his life, he was quoted by John Minford as having confessed to a friend that he was a "Taoist at heart, and I can well believe it, since he was fond of a quiet life, and was free of that extreme form of combative scholarship which seems to be the hall mark of most Sinologists."

NINJUTSU AND THE BOOK OF WAR

A Select Chronology

512 BCE	Sun Tzu authors the ***Bingfa***, later to be titled *The Art of War*
206 BCE	The oldest copy of the *Bingfa* is dated to this time.
735	Kibi-no-Makibi introduces the *Bingfa* to Japan
765	Kibi-no-Makibi begins teaching the principles of the *Bingfa*, now called ***Sonshi-no-Heiho*** in Japan
891	Fujiwara-no-Sukeyo compiles the ***Nihon Genzaisho Mokoroku***, which lists six different editions of the *Sonshi-no-Heiho*.
940	Section of the ***Shomonki*** chronicles the use of secret agents acting in accordance with descriptions found in the *Sonshi*
1171	Minamoto Yoshitsune becomes a student of the *Sonshi* while cloistered on Mount Kurama
1182	Deception strategies used in the *Battle of Yokota ga hara* parallel those found in the *Sonshi*
1336 – 1392	The Nanboku-cho period. The activities of trained spies and assassins start being recorded at this time
1485 – 1581	Greatest level of Ninjutsu activity recorded during the time, particularly involving professional *shinobi* from the Iga and Kouga clans
1467 – 1603	Sengoku period. Clan leaders and daimyo thoroughly versed in Sonbu's teachings and begin training their own *shinobi*

1603	Japan is united, the nation is at peace, and Ninjutsu is outlawed
1655	Hattori Kiyonobu writes the *Ninpiden*
1676	Fujibayashi Yasutake compiles the multi-volume *Bansenshukai*
1681	Natori Masatake writes the *Shoninki*
1772	*Sonshi* translated into a European language for the first time by French Jesuit Jean Joseph Marie Amiot, a chief correspondent with Louis XVI's government on Chinese matters.
1905	The treatise is translated into English for the first time by Captain Everard Ferguson Calthrop, RFA, residing in Tokyo at the time. The work, published as *Sonshi*, was made with the assistance of two Japanese translators.
1908	Calthrop revised the **Sonshi** text in London and publishes it as *The Book of War*
1910	The now familiar English-language version appears, written by Dr. Lionel Giles who chose to title it *The Art of War*. Unlike Calthrop, Giles had no military background, and his work is written primarily for members of the community who held an interest in Chinese language and literature.
1944	The Giles translation is re-edited and published in the United States as part of a series of military science books to be read by members of the Armed Forces
1962	Jay Gluck publishes *Zen Combat*, the first English language book to dedicate a full chapter to the Art of Ninjutsu
1963	The first militarily relevant translation of the text is published by Brigadier General Samuel B. Griffith. This translation was considered more faithful to the original than the Giles translation.

1964	The Art of Ninjutsu is first taught in the United States by Ronald Duncan-sensei in Brooklyn, NY
1970	Andrew Adams publishes *Ninja: The Invisible Assassins*, first English language book expressly dedicated to the Art of Ninjutsu
1981	Stephen K. Hayes publishes *The Ninja and Their Secret Fighting Art*
1983	Author James Clavell publishes new a edition of *The Art of War,* which includes commentary on his filming of the epic *Shogun.*
1988	Thomas Cleary, noted scholar of Asian philosophic writing, publishes his translation of *The Art of War*
1988	The film *Wall Street* is released, with Michael Douglass quoting *The Art of War* throughout the script. He earns an Oscar.
1992	Chin-Ning Chu publishes *Thick Face Black Heart*
2001	The Sopranos television series portrays lead character, Tony Soprano, reading *The Art of War*
2005	Ralph D. Sawyer publishes this translation of *The Art of War*
2010	Chin-Ning Chu publishes *The Art of War for Women*

There have been numerous other translations between the mid-1980s and the present.

About the Translator

Everard Ferguson Calthrop served in the Far East as a language officer observing the Russo-Japanese War. Inevitably he found himself tempted by the previously untranslated writings of Sun Tzu and Wu Tzu. His first essay at translation was issued, perhaps privately, in Tokyo in 1905, followed in 1908 by the issue of this, the first UK edition.

Calthrop also served as Military Attache in Tokio, from 1914 to1915. He later served in the Boer War and the Foreign Service in Japan; he was killed in action at Ypres, having attained the rank of Lieutena.-Colonel.

As a result Lionel Giles, the leading Sinologist of the period, was prompted to produce his own translation in 1910, and in the introduction drew attention to the previous "translation" into French by Père Amiot in 1782, and commented unkindly on Calthrop's work: *"The translator's knowledge of Chinese was far too scanty to fit him to grapple with the manifold difficulties of Sun Tzu."*

This should not to detract from the importance of Calthrop's translation in stimulating interest in this founding text of strategic thought. Genuinely uncommon.

ABOUT THE EDITOR

In 1984, James Loriega founded the **New York Ninpokai**, a training facility which soon came to be regarded as *"the premier academy for the traditional shinobi arts in NYC."* Loriega began his formal ninjutsu training in 1967 with the late Grandmaster Ronald Duncan, the first non-Japanese to teach the shinobi arts in the United States—and the acknowledged *Father of American Ninjutsu*. Though he later trained with other ninjutsu masters, it was from Duncan-sensei that Loriega learned the myriad strategies, tactics, techniques, and disciplines of the ancient *shinobi*.

Loriega holds instructor ranks in Ninjutsu, Jujutsu, and Aikijujutsu, as well as in the Western martial arts of *Savate*, *La Canne*, and *Acero Sevillano*, the latter being an Andalusian edged weapons system.

From 1985 to 1995 Loriega served as the Technical Editor and feature author for **Ninja** magazine. His extensive writings have appeared in mainstream martial arts publications such as *Black Belt*, *Warriors*, *Inside Kung-Fu*, *Soldier of Fortune*, and *Tactical Knives*. His first book, **Sevillian Steel**: *The Traditional Knife Fighting Arts of Spain*, presents an overview of Spanish weapons culture, along with the styles, and strategies of this western martial tradition. Since then, over a dozen other works have followed.

Inquiries for seminars or workshops may be made to:
Ninpokai@aol.com

BIBLIOGRAPHY

Adams, Andrew. **Ninja:** *The Invisible Assassins*. Burbank: Ohara Publications. 1971

Chisholm, Hugh. **The Encyclopædia Britannica**; *A Dictionary of Arts, Sciences, Literature and General Information, 11 Ed.,* Cambridge & New York: University Press. 1910

Cleary, Thomas. **Secrets of the Japanese Art of Warfare:** *An Annotated Translation of Yamamoto Kansuke's Classic Treatise.* Tokyo, Rutland, VT, Singapore: Tuttle Publishing. 2012

Cummins, Antony. **Iga and Koka Ninja Skills:** *The Secret Shinobi Scrolls of Chikamatsu Shigenori*. Gloucestershire, UK: The History Press. 2013

de Bary, Wm. Theodore, et al. **Sources of Japanese Tradition**, *Vol. 1*. New York: Columbia University Press. 2001

Dobson, Sebastian. **Britain and Japan**: *Biographical Portraits*, Vol. VIII. Leiden, The Netherlands: Brill. 2013

Draeger, Donn F. **Asian Fighting Arts**. Tokyo, New York, San Francisco: Kodansha International, Ltd. 1969

– **Ninjutsu:** *The Art of Invisibility*. Tokyo: Lotus Press. 1971

– **Classical Bujutsu**. New York & Tokyo: Weatherhill. 1973

Dulles, Allen. **The Craft of Intelligence**. New York: Harper & Row, 1963.

Fujita, Seiko. **What Is Ninjutsu?** Trans. Eric Shahan. CreateSpace. 2017

Gluck, Jay. **Zen Combat**. New York: Ballantine Books. 1962

Inoue Yasushi. **The Samurai Banner of Furin Kazan**. North Clarendon, VT: Tuttle Publishing. 2004.

Loriega, James. **Ninso:** *Ninjutsu's Art of Face Reading*. New York: Pay-Per-Cut Press. 2017

– **The Serpent and the Dove:** *The Shinobi Wisdom of Baltasar Gracián*. New York: Pay-Per- Cut Press. 2017

– **Shinobi-no-Michi:** *The Way of the Ninja*. New York: Lost Arts Publications. 2018

Smith, Robert W. (writing as John F. Gilbey) **Secret Fighting Arts of the World**. Rutland, VT and Tokyo, Japan: Charles E. Tuttle, Inc. 1963

Sun Tzu. **The Art of War**. Edited by James Clavell. New York: Delacorte Press. 1983

Sun Tzu. **The Art of War**. Trans. Lionel Giles. London: Lozac. 1910

Sun Tzu. **The Art of War**. Trans. Samuel Griffith. London: Oxford University Press, 1963

Turnbull, Stephen. **Ninja,** *he True Story of Japan's Secret Warrior Cult*. United Kingdom: Firebird Books. 1991